HOW CAN I AIM TO PLEASE GOD
IN EVERYTHING?

✘ CULTIVATING BIBLICAL GODLINESS

Series Editors

Joel R. Beeke and Ryan M. McGraw

Dr. D. Martyn Lloyd-Jones once said that what the church needs to do most of all is "to begin herself to live the Christian life. If she did that, men and women would be crowding into our buildings. They would say, 'What is the secret of this?'" As Christians, one of our greatest needs is for the Spirit of God to cultivate biblical godliness in us in order to put the beauty of Christ on display through us, all to the glory of the triune God. With this goal in mind, this series of booklets treats matters vital to Christian experience at a basic level. Each booklet addresses a specific question in order to inform the mind, warm the affections, and transform the whole person by the Spirit's grace, so that the church may adorn the doctrine of God our Savior in all things.

HOW CAN I AIM TO PLEASE GOD
IN EVERYTHING?

GEOFFREY THOMAS

REFORMATION HERITAGE BOOKS
GRAND RAPIDS, MICHIGAN

How Can I Aim to Please God in Everything?
© 2019 by Geoffrey Thomas

Reformation Heritage Books
2965 Leonard St. NE
Grand Rapids, MI 49525
616-977-0889
orders@heritagebooks.org
www.heritagebooks.org

Printed in the United States of America
19 20 21 22 23 24/10 9 8 7 6 5 4 3 2 1

ISBN 978-1-60178-698-2
ISBN 978-1-60178-699-9 (e-pub)

For additional Reformed literature, request a free book list from Reformation Heritage Books at the above regular or e-mail address.

HOW CAN I AIM TO PLEASE GOD
IN EVERYTHING?

———— ✳ ————

Therefore we are always confident, knowing that, whilst we are at home in the body, we are absent from the Lord: (for we walk by faith, not by sight:) we are confident, I say, and willing rather to be absent from the body, and to be present with the Lord. Wherefore we labour, that, whether present or absent, we may be accepted of him.

—2 Corinthians 5:6–9

The goal of every Christian is to please God in everything at all times. Nothing can compromise this ambition. In all I do—eating, drinking, working, resting—my aim is to please and glorify God. I cannot be selective—not pleasing Him sometimes or in many ways. Rather, this is my prayer: "Take my whole life and it will be ever, only, all for Thee." Christ's apostle Paul says, "Wherefore we labour, that, whether present or absent, we may be accepted of him" (2 Cor. 5:9). In other words, we want God's will on earth as much as we know we are going to want it when we will be in heaven before Him.

Christians have a strange kind of certainty that while they live in this world they are actually away from the Lord. Paul says it so starkly: "We are always confident, knowing that, whilst we are at home in the body, we are absent from the Lord" (2 Cor. 5:6). He tells us that he is quite sure about this fact. We might protest that Christ has promised "I am with you always" (Matt. 28:20), and He has affirmed that "where two or three are gathered together in my name, there am I in the midst of them" (Matt. 18:20). Is there a single time or place or any activity in which we are engaged when we are absolutely by ourselves, without the Lord? No, He is always with us, as He will be with us at the very end when we walk through the valley of the shadow of death. All that is true. What a precious confidence that gives to us! Because He is God the Son, He is omnipresent, and so we are never away from the Lord for a single moment. Illimitable access to the indwelling Savior makes it possible for us always to please God in everything we do. There is no hope without that. We can do all things required of us only through Christ who strengthens us.

But the Lord Jesus Christ is no longer in the world. He was in the world, and one day He will be returning to the world, but now He has ascended to heaven. He made that very clear, saying, "I leave the world, and go to the Father" (John 16:28), and again, "Now I am no more in the world" (John 17:11). God sent two messengers to tell this to the early church: "This same Jesus…is taken up from you into heaven" (Acts 1:11). We know where the Lord Jesus is today. He has taken His seat at "the right hand of the Majesty on high" (Heb. 1:3), "now to appear in the presence of God for us" (Heb. 9:24). His intercession and reign at God's right hand with all heavenly and earthly authority is the source of all our strength always and everywhere to please Him.

So the apostle is absolutely right: while we followers of the Lord must remain in the world, the man Christ Jesus is not in the world. We have to live without the sight of His physical presence every day of our lives. We do not apologize for this or try to hide that from the young Christian. We are quite certain about it, and we tell everyone that "whilst we are at home in the body, we are absent from the Lord" (2 Cor. 5:6). We have to live our lives as Christians without any sound or aroma or taste or touch or sight of the physical body of the Lord Jesus. He has a body that must be in one place, and it can and will be in that one place exclusively and forever, and that place is not this world. It is never in this world. We would be denying the physical nature of the resurrection if we even thought that the Lord Jesus was prone to make occasional bodily visits to this planet—like some extraterrestrial who drops down. If you think you are seeing what you consider to be a vision of Jesus, reject it. Luther thought that apparitions of

Jesus were more dangerous than those of the devil, at whom He threw an ink pot. The whole church has to be away from the risen and ascended and enthroned Jesus Christ all the centuries we are in these mortal bodies. But that is no handicap to our pleasing God always and everywhere.

I must go on to insist that the Son of God is also always with us. He indwells us by His Spirit; He speaks to us by His Word and so teaches us as our prophet; He directs us according to His providence and protects us daily as our shepherd. He is head of the church and head of all things for our sake. He sympathizes with our grief and sends relief to needy sufferers. There are such constant dynamics in the living and growing relationship that we have with Him, but we constantly bear in mind that always we have to be "away from the Lord." We do not use disturbing nebulous language claiming that in times of great spiritual awakening the man Christ Jesus for a moment stepped down from the throne of the universe and bodily came to some insignificant Welsh village or appeared to a peasant girl in Spain or France. How in the world does anyone know that? Let the Roman Catholics tell their fairy stories. We never want the Lord Jesus to leave His throne until all His work is done. We cry out, "Reign on, King of kings and Lord of lords and only Ruler of princes! Don't move from that place, but do send Thy Spirit forth upon us!" We are always confident and know that the God-man remains seated at the Father's right hand with all authority in heaven and earth.

There He will remain until the day of His second coming, when He will return to this planet, and all His holy angels with Him, to raise the dead and set up the judgment throne. That is the next time people will see Him on this earth. But we also know that from the throne He sends forth the Spirit. Peter declares at Pentecost that "being by the right hand of God exalted, and having received of the Father the promise of the Holy Ghost, he hath shed forth this, which ye now see and hear" (Acts 2:33). Peter did not cry out, "Jesus is here!" He said that He was *there*—exalted to the right hand of God—and that He had from heaven poured out what they were seeing and hearing at Pentecost. The Lord Jesus has been doing that for the last two thousand years. He is the one who made us Christians through sending His Spirit to us in regeneration, giving us saving faith and repentance; and we long for Him to pour out His Spirit in more abundance on the earth, on multitudes of favored men and women during our lifetimes. Only by Him can we please God everywhere and in all things.

So the apostle Paul, like every one of us, was away from the Lord, though this separation was not his preference. He desired "rather to be absent from the body, and to be present with the Lord" (2 Cor. 5:8), and as Christians mature they can enter more into that longing for death and the glorious life that lies beyond that. They groan with the apostle and earnestly desire their heavenly resurrected bodies in glory. There will be no partings there, and no suffering, and no sin. We would prefer to be away from these lowly bodies and get home to our Savior. But God's decree is that all Christians must live their life in this world "away from the Lord," and in everything and in all things we have to live our daily lives as Christians without sight or sound of the Lord Jesus. How do we do so?

WE LIVE BY FAITH

"We walk by faith, not by sight" (2 Cor. 5:7). Those one-syllable words—how simple each one is—and yet all the challenge of Christian discipleship is in them. True happiness and contentment is found by trusting in God, and not by sight. We may always live God-glorifying lives without a sight of Christ because we live trusting God's promises. Faith is a connecting grace. It joins us to the Son of God. It plugs us into His energy and graces. We become united to Him, and thus His life flows into us. What does it mean to live like that?

First, to live by faith requires us to know what we are to believe. Paul asks that great question, "How shall they believe in him of whom they have not heard?" (Rom. 10:14). A street urchin may only know the words "Jesus" or "Christ" as oaths. He knows nothing at all about the Savior, just those swear words, so he needs knowledge of who the Lord is.

He will never live for the Lord until he knows the identity of the Lord. You have to tell him that once a man walked this earth, and the winds and the waves obeyed Him. The sick came to Him, and He healed every one of them. He claimed that He was the incarnate God—"I and my Father are one" (John 10:30). He told people that He had come into the world not to receive service from them but to serve, and the greatest service He performed was to die, paying our ransom price and thus purchasing our freedom from sin's lordship over us. He came from heaven as the Son of God to search for sinners and to save them by becoming the Lamb of God dealing with the world's sin. Almighty God actually laid on Him the iniquity of all His people. Jesus paid the wages of sin in our place. He bore our own condemnation in His body on Golgotha's cross.

> Because the sinless Savior died,
> My sinful soul is counted free.
> For God, the just, is satisfied
> To look on Him and pardon me.[1]

We know that this is so because of one great event in history when God raised Jesus from the dead on the third day. So there is forgiveness and sonship and new life found through trusting in Jesus Christ. We tell the world all we can and all that they will

---

1. Charitie L. Bancroft, "Before the Throne of God Above," in the public domain.

receive of the teaching and activities of the extraordinary life of the Lord Jesus Christ.

That is the sort of knowledge we want men and women to have. We start by giving them information about the living God by every legitimate means. There are long-term evangelistic activities that every Christian church engages in. We may display a verse from the Bible outside our building. We may distribute calendars with texts for each month or a church leaflet. We may give to an individual a pamphlet, a book, a gospel, a New Testament, a Bible, a book of sermons of Martyn Lloyd-Jones—even a tome refuting atheism. We are to be thoughtful and flexible about the materials we distribute, but we have to spread abroad the knowledge of God. We organize Sunday schools, children's meetings, young people's meetings, and men's and women's meetings. There are special events, but above all we preach the Bible at every service. Our first responsibility is to teach the rudiments of Christianity and to live out the Christian message by consistent, loving, and God-fearing lives.

> May His beauty rest upon me
> As I seek the lost to win,
> And may they forget the channel,
> Seeing only Him.[2]

---

2. Kate B. Wilkinson, "May the Mind of Christ, My Savior," in the public domain.

Before pagans can live by faith they must know who the Lord Jesus is, what He has done, and what are the blessings God promises to give. Consider the humble tract. I once stood next to the late Des Roberts of Swansea at his post outside the city market on a Saturday afternoon, watching him handing out tracts as he had done for forty years. I worked out that he has distributed about one and three-quarter million tracts during that time, giving the people of Swansea the knowledge of who Christ is. How can they live by faith if they do not know the One in whom they are to place their faith?

In the story of William Gibson Sloan, the missionary fisherman to the Faroe Islands, Fred Kelling, Sloan's biographer, writes about the last week of the evangelist's life and a young man to whom Sloan often witnessed, who said, "Always he spoke to me about eternity, and of how much the Lord Jesus loved sinners like me; but I only laughed at him and didn't want to be affected by what he said." It was late one evening after their conversation as these two men, the preacher and the scoffer, were walking to their homes on different sides of the street. Sloan was going on his way with a handful of tracts, and he was giving them out to people who walked toward him on the road. His eyesight was failing, and it was getting dark. Sloan spotted what he thought was a person standing by the roadside, so he moved across the pavement with a tract in an outstretched hand, but he discovered that it was merely a stone pillar.

The young man was watching all this from across the road, and the incident made a deep impression on him. He said,

> When I saw this, it was as if I had been struck by lightning. I thought to myself, "You are just like that rock. Just as dead, cold and hard as that stone." As I followed that old warrior of the Lord Jesus Christ to his home, it came to me with tremendous force how necessary it was for me to be saved, and how dangerous it is to harden your heart against the calling of the Spirit.

Two days later, September 4, 1914, William Sloan died, but not before the young man had told him, "I too am saved, and have found forgiveness of sins, peace, and eternal life through the finished work of the Lord Jesus Christ."[3] To live by faith people must have information about the One they must believe in, and the very manner in which we give that knowledge to them can be as important as the message itself.

Second, to live by faith requires us to conclude that what we have come to know is true. We have to give our assent to the gospel's veracity. Take this great statement: "Jesus of Nazareth is the long-promised Messiah." Paul had to defend and demonstrate that this assertion was true from the Scriptures as he presented it to his hearers in the synagogues.

---

3. Fred Kelling, *Fisherman of Faroe: William Gibson Sloan* (Gota, Faroe Islands: Leirkerid Publications, 1993), 232.

He couldn't shout out, "Jesus is the Christ!" and expect them all to say, "Amen!" We are told this:

> Paul, as his manner was, went in unto them, and three sabbath days reasoned with them out of the scriptures, opening and alleging, that Christ must needs have suffered, and risen again from the dead; and that this Jesus, whom I preach unto you, is Christ. And some of them believed, and consorted with Paul and Silas. (Acts 17:2–4)

Paul did not bomb them with one explosive statement after another and then stand back to see what effect his words had. He explained the Scriptures and reasoned with them and sought to persuade them that the gospel was true. That is Christian evangelism. The apostle writes from prison and says that he was put there for "the defence and confirmation of the gospel" (Phil. 1:7). Much of the preaching in the book of Acts and the letters written in the New Testament are for the defense of the gospel.

At Pentecost, Peter defended the gospel from the claim that its preachers were drunk. Paul wrote to the Galatians to defend the truth of the gospel of God's grace. They both sought to remove every excuse and obstacle that men and women plead to excuse their disbelief of the Christian message.

In the centenary story of the Rosskeen church in the north of Scotland, Janice MacLellan narrates how she came to live by faith. She came from a completely nonchurch-going stock—in fact, from a New

Age background. She was drawn to the Rosskeen church by remarks she heard that their preacher was good, and she was impressed by the number of cars parked outside the church building. She visited initially at a time of personal loss in her life. As the months went by, she came under growing persuasion that what she was hearing was God's message. She and her boyfriend were living together, and after some time in the fellowship they decided that they had to get married, so they spoke to the minister, Kenny MacDonald, about it. One evening a week or so later, MacLellan recounts, they were arranging the wedding, and the minister asked the couple:

> "How is your relationship with God?" Stumbling over my words, I replied, "We don't really have one, but we want one." "Keep your eyes on Jesus," was his simple answer. As we drove home, I pondered what he had said: "What had Jesus done for me?" As I asked the question, an image of a man on a cross burned into my mind. Just like that—quite simply, no emotion, just my answer, "Jesus died on the cross for my sins. That was how everything could be made right with my Heavenly Father—Jesus had paid the price for my sins, instead of me. I was free!"[4]

---

4. Janice MacLellan, *Ordinary People, Extraordinary God: Celebrating 100 Years of God at Work in Rosskeen Free Church* (Fearn, Scotland: Christian Focus, 2000), 124.

She heard the message about Jesus, and then she came to realize it was true. He had paid the price for her sins, and she was free. We must know the contents of the gospel of Jesus, but we must agree to the truthfulness of the message if we are going to live by it.

Third, to live by faith is to wholly commit ourselves in everything and at all times to the One we have come to know as the living God. It is essential to know the message. How can we believe in Jesus without hearing about Him? But knowledge alone is not enough. We must go on to acknowledge, "This Christian message is true." But just assenting to its truth is not enough. The devils believe that Christianity is true. We have to go further and deeper, entrusting ourselves, body and soul, for time and eternity to this faithful Savior, Jesus Christ alone. There is no other way that we can live by faith.

There is a famous incident in the life of John G. Paton, a nineteenth-century missionary to the South Pacific. He was engaged in translating the Bible into the language of the people, but he found that he couldn't find a word in their vocabulary to express the concept of *faith*. He was sitting in his room, and one of the local Christians came in and said to him something like, "You're sitting down today?" Paton knew the phrase, and then he changed his posture, leaning hard against the back of the chair, and he turned to the man and asked him, "Now what am I doing?" The man said in the language of the people,

"You are resting your weight on the chair back." Paton was entrusting himself to that chair to hold him up and support him. It was a vivid word, and Paton was delighted to get it because it was a splendid translation of the New Testament term to "trust in" someone.[5] You rest your entire self on Jesus Christ. You lean exclusively without depending in the least on any resources of your own—not that you have any such resources. You must confess, "I will trust in God. I will trust without depending in the least on anything else." Read through that great hymn "Take My Life and Let It Be" by Frances Ridley Havergal. It describes saving trust in Christ. Start at the end:

> Take myself, and I will be
> Ever, only, all, for Thee.[6]

Then work your way through the commitment of every part of yourself, giving everything to the Lord: "Take my moments and my days...my hands...my feet...my voice...my lips...my silver and my gold... my intellect...my will...my heart...my love." That is salvation. To trust is the first act of a newborn soul: "I will trust Him." If you do not trust God for your

---

5. *John G. Paton, Missionary to the New Hebrides: An Autobiography* (London: Banner of Truth, 1965). http://www.alfredplacechurch.org .uk/index.php/sermons/2-corinthians/56-9-how-christians-live-their -lives/

6. Frances Ridley Havergal, "Take My Life and Let It Be," in the public domain.

salvation, you are not a Christian. The first thing you do in becoming a follower of Christ is to entrust yourself to Him. You cease trusting in your own hunches, your own feelings, your own good life, your own religion, your own faith. You cease trusting in your praying.

There was a fine Christian man on the island of Lewis named Norman MacDonald. He was born in 1853, and throughout his Christian life he was known as Happy Norman. He had made a sort of profession as a teenager, but he quickly forsook the Lord he had once acknowledged. He went back into the world. He still continued to pray, but looking back, he had no happiness about that praying. He said, "When I was young I expected to be saved because I was able to pray, but I discovered at the last that in my prayers I was giving the first place to the world, the second to myself, and the tail of it to the Lord." You do not trust in the exercises of religion, in the hand of the bishop on your head, or going to Mass or Holy Communion, or in your ability to pray. You make a bundle of all that religious activity and flee from it all to trust solely and exclusively in the Lord Jesus Christ.

Consider how this assurance of trusting in Christ's grace alone came to one young man. In the year of the French Revolution, 1789, an eighteen-year-old American named Archibald Alexander was climbing the long slope of a hill near the town of Lexington, Virginia. He had a Bible in his hand, and he came to a large rock on the side of the forested hill where he knelt and prayed for his own salvation. He had been in deep spiritual struggle of soul for months.

> He wished to have the conscious feeling within his own heart that his soul was redeemed. Then a passage was read from the Bible and another prayer was offered. Thus he read the Word and prayed, and read and prayed again and again until his strength was gone, for the young man had not tasted food that day. Weak as he was and in despair it seemed to him that God would not hear him. His own heart seemed to him to become harder and more and more devoid of every serious emotion. He knelt again on the ground and uttered one broken cry for help, "when, in a moment," he tells us, "I had such an inner view of a crucified Saviour as has been without a parallel in my experience." He went on to say, "The whole plan of grace appeared as clear as day. I was persuaded that God was willing to accept me, just as I was, and convinced that I had never before understood the freeness of salvation, but had always been striving to bring some price in my hand, or to prepare myself for receiving Christ. Now I discovered that I could receive him in all his offices at that very moment, which I was sure at the time I did. I felt truly a joy which was unspeakable and full of glory."[7]

---

7. Henry Alexander White, *Southern Presbyterian Leaders 1683–1911* (Edinburgh: Banner of Truth, 2000), 181–82.

When God gives you grace to put your trust solely in the living God, you come to an assurance that He has accepted you for the sake of Jesus only. You trust in the blood of Jesus, who bore your punishment on the cross, and you believe that because He became the sin-bearing Lamb, you will not bear any condemnation. That is trusting God. That is the beginning of living by faith, and you never want to move from that place for a single day of your life.

In summary, you are never going to see Jesus Christ with your eyes while you are at home in the body, so you daily live, trusting in Him. So saving faith is grasping real knowledge. Personal saving faith is believing the truth for yourself. Saving faith is entrusting all of yourself to all of Christ—the Prophet who teaches you, the Priest who ever lives to intercede for you, and the King who protects and governs you. That is living by faith and not by sight.

WE MAKE IT OUR GOAL TO PLEASE HIM IN EVERYTHING

"Wherefore we labour, that, whether present or absent, we may be accepted of him" (2 Cor. 5:9). This theme is often emphasized in Scripture. Paul prays for the Colossians that they may please the Lord in every way (Col. 1:10). He reminds the Thessalonians of his purpose in teaching them: "Ye have received of us how ye ought to walk and to please God" (1 Thess. 4:1). He tells Timothy how widows should behave, and he says "that is good and acceptable before God"

(1 Tim. 5:4). He exhorts the Ephesians to be "proving what is acceptable unto the Lord" (Eph. 5:10).

A Christian is a person whose desire—everywhere and always—is to please God, his loving Father. On the day of Pentecost Peter quotes David: "I foresaw the Lord always before my face, for he is on my right hand, that I should not be moved" (Acts 2:25). That is a Christian. By grace, His eyes are on the face of his Master. We occasionally hear, for example, of someone being described as a "born-again Christian." But this is a repetition of words. What other kind of Christian is there? One cannot be an unborn-again Christian. To belong to the generation of the once-born, to be born only of nature and of blood and of the will of man is not to be a Christian at all. A person cannot be a child of God at all until he or she has been born twice and entered into a saving, evangelical experience of divine grace.

In the same way, just as "born-again Christian" is a needless multiplicity of words, so also is the description "committed Christian." What other kind of Christian is there? Can one be an "uncommitted" Christian? Surely if a person is unsurrendered, unyielded, and unavailable for the Master's use, one has every right to question whether he or she is a Christian at all. God once said about the Northern Kingdom of Israel, "Ephraim is a cake not turned" (Hos. 7:8). Today we would say a half-baked pancake, raw on one side and cooked on the other, is inedible and useless. You are either saved or lost, either for

Jesus or against Him, either seeking to please Him in all things or you are not. A genuine disciple asks, How can I please the Lord whether I live or die? That is one of the most important questions in life.

In *The Cost of Commitment*, author John White cites a letter written by an American Marxist in Mexico City in which he breaks off his engagement with his fiancée:

> We Marxists suffer many casualties. We are those whom they shoot, hang, lynch, tar and feather, imprison, slander, fire from our jobs and whose lives people make miserable in every way possible. We live in poverty. From what we earn we turn over to the Party every cent which we do not absolutely need to live. We communists have neither time nor money for concerts, nor for beautiful homes and new cars. They call us fanatics. We are fanatics. Our lives are dominated by one supreme factor—the struggle for world communism. We communists have a philosophy of life that money could not buy.
>
> We have a cause to fight for, a specific goal in life. We lost our insignificant identities in the great river of humanity; and if our personal lives seem hard, or if our egos seem bruised through subordination to the Party, we are amply rewarded in the thought that all of us, even though it be in a very small way, are contributing something new and better for humanity.
>
> There is one thing about which I am completely in earnest—the communist cause. It is my life, my business, my religion, my hobby,

my sweetheart, my wife, my mistress, my meat
and drink. I work at it by day and dream of it
by night. Its control over me grows greater with
the passage of time. Therefore I cannot have a
friend, a lover, or even a conversation without
relating them to this power that animates and
controls my life. I measure people, books, ideas,
and deeds according to the way they affect the
communist cause and by their attitude to it. I
have already been in jail for my ideas, and if
need be, I am ready to face death.[8]

That is a man whose one goal in life is to serve
the cause of Karl Marx. Our goal is to please the Savior who gave Himself for us always and everywhere.
What are some of the ways we real Christians please
the God we profess to know and love? Let me select
four examples out of many.

First, we please the Lord by our evangelistic compassion. We are told of the Lord Jesus that when He
saw the multitudes He had compassion on them, for
they were like sheep without a shepherd. This is the
attitude that pleases God. Hudson Taylor was the
father of the evangelism of China, but before he left
England he found his own heart growing increas-
ingly compassionate for sinners. It was not a trip
overseas that made him a missionary. In the year
1853 he was twenty-one years of age and assisting a

London doctor, going to his patients in their homes and helping them. There was one man who had senile gangrene with no hope of recovery, and every day Taylor went to his home to dress the wound. The man was a committed atheist. He would allow no one to speak to him about religion, and when the local vicar called he spat in his face. His temper was not under control, and he was a very violent man. How did Taylor react to this man? These are his words:

> Upon first commencing to attend him I prayed much about it, but for two or three days said nothing of a religious nature. By special care in dressing his diseased limb I was able considerably to lessen his sufferings, and he soon began to manifest appreciation of my services. One day with a trembling heart I took advantage of his grateful acknowledgements to tell him what was the spring of my action, and to speak of his solemn position and need of God's mercy through Christ. It was evidently only a powerful effort of self-restraint that kept his lips closed. He turned over in bed with his back to me, and uttered no word.
>
> I could not get the poor man out of my mind, and very often through each day I pleaded with God, by his Spirit, to save him ere he took him hence. After dressing the wound and relieving the pain, I never failed to say a few words to him which I hoped the Lord would bless. He always turned his back looking annoyed, but never made any reply.

After continuing this for some time my heart sank. It seemed to me that I was not only doing no good but perhaps really hardening him and increasing his guilt. One day after dressing his limb and washing my hands, instead of returning to the bedside, I went to the door and stood hesitating a moment with the thought in my mind, "Ephraim is joined to his idols, let him alone." Looking at my patient I saw his surprise, as it was the first time since opening the subject that I had attempted to leave without saying a few words for my Master.

I could bear it no longer. Bursting into tears, I crossed the room and said: "My friend, whether you will hear or whether you will forbear, I must deliver my soul," and went on to speak very earnestly, telling him how much I wished that he would let me pray with him. To my unspeakable joy he did not turn away, but replied: "If it will be a relief to you, do." I need scarcely say that falling upon my knees I poured out my soul to God on his behalf. Then and there, I believe, the Lord wrought a change in his soul.

He was never afterwards unwilling to be spoken to and prayed with, and within a few days he definitely accepted Christ as his Savior.

Oh the joy it was to me to see that man rejoicing in hope of the glory of God. He told me that for forty years he had never darkened the door of a church or chapel, and that then, forty years ago, he had only entered a place of worship to be married, and could not be persuaded to go inside even when his wife was buried. Now, thank God, I had every reason to believe his sin-stained soul was washed, was sanctified, was "justified, in the Name of the Lord Jesus and by the Spirit of our God." Often in my early work in China, when circumstances rendered me almost hopeless of success, I have thought of this man's conversion and have been encouraged to persevere in speaking the Word, whether men would hear or whether they would forbear. The now happy sufferer lived for some time after this change, and was never tired of bearing testimony to the grace of God.[9]

How pleasing to the Lord was Hudson Taylor's compassion, perseverance, and courage!

Second, we please the Lord by doing our daily work to His glory. Every day we seek to please Him, not just in evangelism but in our vocation, whether we are a housewife and mother, or a student, or if we have retired from our regular work. We want to please the Lord in how we do our duties each day. William Tyndale said that if we look externally "there is difference betwixt washing of dishes and preaching the word of God; but as touching to please God, none at all."[10] William Perkins said, "The action of a shepherd in keeping sheep...is as good a

---

9. Dr. and Mrs. Howard Taylor, *Hudson Taylor in Early Years: The Growth of a Soul* (New York: Hodder & Stoughton, 1912), 179–80.

10. Cited in Timothy George, *Theology of the Reformers* (Nashville: Broadman, 1988), 370.

work before God as is the action of a judge in giving the sentence, or a magistrate in ruling, or a minister in preaching."[11] Some of you who are reading these words have supervisors over you who are demanding, pointing out your every failure or mistake, even imagined ones, and never praising you for anything done well. To think that soon you will be back in the office, or teaching in the school, or working at the factory fills you with apprehension, but please hear me, it is possible for you in that place to please the Lord and know His blessing. Pay attention to Paul as he exhorts Christian slaves about their duties:

> Servants, be obedient to them that are your masters according to the flesh, with fear and trembling, in singleness of your heart, as unto Christ; not with eyeservice, as menpleasers; but as the servants of Christ, doing the will of God from the heart; with good will doing service, as to the Lord, and not to men: knowing that whatsoever good thing any man doeth, the same shall he receive of the Lord, whether he be bond or free. (Eph. 6:5–8)

How do you win your masters for Jesus Christ if you are dishonest, lazy, rude, and threatening to them? You win them without the word when they can see that your life is different from the life of every other slave in the house. When Joseph was a

---

11. Cited in Leland Ryken, *Worldly Saints: The Puritans as They Really Were* (Grand Rapids: Zondervan, 2014), 25.

slave in Egypt working for Potiphar, he had the Lord with him and he prospered. The Lord gave him success in everything he did. Joseph was promoted, and "the blessing of the LORD was upon all that he had in the house, and in the field" (Gen. 39:5). Isn't that what we want? The Lord's blessing on us in school, in the shop, in business, repairing burst pipes, fixing lawn mowers, washing our family's clothes—the Lord being with us and giving us success? Without the Word of God, our employers are changed by how we live to please God. We do our daily work for His sake. This conviction brings divinity to drudgery. We do everything with all our might—whatever our hands pick up. How pleasing to the Lord was Joseph's daily work as a slave.

Third, we please the Lord by keeping the Lord's Day special. You remember that there was a pattern to the weekly life of our Lord. We are told that He had just one "custom," and He invariably kept it without exception, and that was to attend the place of worship and biblical instruction one whole day in every seven (Luke 4:16). Now we please the same Lord if we also keep that pattern for our weeks and years. Sundays are different for us. Once a week an opportunity is given to us to gather with other Christians and be taught the Word of God, to witness a baptismal service that we will never forget, to break bread around the Communion table, and we encourage other Christians by spending time with them, showing our affection for them.

On Sundays the house is quiet, the computer is shut down, the clothes remain unwashed and unironed, the car stays dirty, the weeds can grow in the garden, our textbooks on mathematics and literature and the history of the Napoleonic wars remain unstudied, and our dissertation on economics or international politics is unwritten. We spend the day with other followers of the Lord Jesus, pleasing Him by our custom of meeting with other Christians and worshiping God. That delights our Lord.

Fourth, we please the Lord by having a Christian home. God invented the family. If unfallen Adam could have been quite happy by himself and thought, "I like my space," God would have shaken His head, saying, "No! That is not good for you. I have made you for communication and relationships and sharing and personal affection, as I love My Son and the Spirit." There was at that time no sin in the world, and though man had the daily delight of personal communication with God, it was still not good for man to be a loner. Nothing has changed. You need help from someone else. You rely on someone else to get through life, and there is someone who is relying on you, even if you are available only through a telephone or text messages. Independence doesn't please the Lord. There is the Clint Eastwood figure of the man without a name, the lone avenger who comes into a town, sorts everything out, and then rides off alone into the sunset—that is not a good role model. Neither the Levite walking by the hurting man nor the priest walking past him pleased the Lord. The one who stopped and got involved with the man in his pain, who made provision for his future, pleased the Lord. Marriage requires much stopping and helping and planning ahead. Sometimes it is the husband stopping and helping, and sometimes it is the wife. Marriage requires much caring and cherishing. Marriage is a husband and a wife raising children together. Marriage is two people putting toast in the toaster for each other, sharing a meal together.

Marriage is two people particularly sharing in everything in their lives with just one other special person of the opposite sex. Marriage is a man saying, "I love you so much that I don't want to go to bed with you just tonight, but I want to share a bed with you alone and no one else for the rest of my life, until death us do part. That is how much I love you." That is the promise the husband makes: "I'll always be around to look after any children that the Lord gives us." And that sharing of our bodies is in the context of sharing our money, frustrations, possessions, grandchildren, senility, in-laws, and deaths. We are one. And when the husband loves his wife so much that he would give his life for her and nourishes and cherishes her, then he is showing something of Christ's love. And the same tender, true love and submission is also to be shown by the wife. That is a Christian home that pleases the Lord.

So Paul is showing us how we may please God always and everywhere. First, we live by faith, and second, we make it our goal to glorify the Lord in all of this life (and I have given you four concrete examples of that), as much as we know we shall also in the life to come. That is how Christians, despite their weaknesses and failings, strive to live their daily lives.